Luv, Lucas
by Gregory Joseph Borowski

Acknowledgement
I would like to express my gratitude to Dr. Ben Carlsen, Clarence Atkins, Lize-Marie Ergur and Goksun Ergur for their love, support and sound advice. Your friendship and guidance raising a very special dog made this book possible.

Follow us on social media!
Luv Lucas  **#luvlucas**

This edition published by **Flying Page Publishing**
flyingpagepublishing.com

ISBN: 978-1-63649-168-4

Library of Congress Control Number: 2020919019

Hi! My name is Lucas.
Like you, I started out small.
Everything was big and
new around me. Growing up,
I soon found out that
learning about life was fun.
Here are some learnings
I found along the way!

I don't have to know
everything all at once.
Life will teach me as
I go along.

When I was a baby
I didn't learn yet that
sharing feels good.

I just like to smile.
Smiling is my favorite
thing to do.

It's always the right
time to try new things.

Being in nature reminds
me that something amazing
is about to happen.

My to do list every day:
Smile, be happy,
and always find time
to play!

I'm always ready for
the ride of a lifetime.

I can only have one
thought at a time so
I might as well make it
a good one.

I try to pay attention.
It lets others know I care.

I'm shining my light so
bright today.
Sunglasses required.

If it's a gift,
deal with it. It came
from someone's heart.

My favorite kind
of smell is the smell
of fresh air.

I love to look at
everything like I'm seeing
it for the first time.

If it makes someone
happy, do it!

When I watch the
raindrops I know the
next sunny day is
waiting to happen.

My best friend knows how
to have fun, and accepts
me just the way I am.

Patience is a virtue.
Pizza is better.

Sometimes just
being close to each other
is enough.

When I explore the
world out there, I find all
sorts of big and small
adventures.

I always expect a
happy moment.

When I really like
something, I hang on
and don't let go.

I'm all grown up now and have a job. I go to hospitals and schools and get many hugs. I'm saving one big hug for you. Thank you for being my special friend!

Luv,
Lucas

Life is a circle of learning

We are learning all the time; from each other, from our animal friends and from nature's wonders. When we learn something helpful it's ours to share with the world around us. As we share with kindness, the cycle continues, circles back to us and gives us another opportunity to grow.

CPSIA information can be obtained
at www.ICGtesting.com
Printed in the USA
LVHW011035041220
672129LV00036B/934